The lost teddy

Written and illustrated by

David Bennett

Conran Octopus

Here is Ben and the Baby Gang.
They are going to play hospitals.
'Dot's very ill,' said Kate.
'Scruff's not well either,' said Ben.

Lucy and Woolly have got their toys too.
But Sam can't find his anywhere.
'I've lost my dancing teddy,' he cried.
'Come and help me look for him.'

The Gang looked under the bed.
Out jumped Candy, the cat.
'Teddy's not here,' said Kate, sadly.

They opened the cupboard.
Out fell lots of toys.
'He's not here, either,' shouted Sam.
'Oh, where can he be?'

'Maybe he's gone to the beach
for a swim,' said Kate.

‘I bet he’s gone dancing again,’
said Sam.

While the others were thinking,
Lucy crawled out of the room.

Only Woolly saw her go.

Woolly ran up to Ben and
tugged at his trousers.
'Go away, you silly dog,'
said Ben, crossly.

‘He wants you to follow him,’
laughed Kate.
‘Maybe he knows where
your teddy is hiding!’

Ben, Sam and Kate followed Woolly
into the garden.
And there, all alone, sat Lucy.

' 'ook,' she babbled, pointing at the sky.
Sam and the Gang looked up as well.
And guess what they saw?

Hanging up on the clothes line
was Sam's dancing teddy.
'There's my poor teddy,' he shouted.
'Mum's washed him again.'

‘I’ll get him down for you,’ said Ben,
standing on tiptoes.
But teddy was much too high
for him to reach.

‘You try, Kate,’ said Ben,
crouching down on the grass.
Kate climbed on his back.

‘It’s no good,’ said Kate,
‘I can’t get him either.’

‘I’ve got an idea,’ said Ben.
‘Let’s use Dad’s wheelbarrow.’
‘We’ll help you push it,’
said Kate and Sam.

Ben stood in the wheelbarrow
and grabbed hold of the teddy.
He pulled and he pulled
and he pulled.

TWANG! went the clothes line.
Down tumbled Sam's teddy
and all the clean washing.

It fell right on top of
Ben and the Gang.

Sam picked up his teddy and gave him a hug.
'Follow me, Gang,' he shouted.
'Now teddy can join in our hospital game.'

‘Teddy can be the patient,’ said Sam,
‘because he’s had a big fall.’
‘Scruff can be the doctor,’ said Ben.
‘And Dot can be the nurse,’ laughed Kate.

After the game was over,
Sam kissed his teddy.
'Don't ever get lost again,'
he whispered into his ear.

Designed by David Bennett

Typeset in Helvetica Regular 18pt
by Type City Limited
Printed by Eagle Press, Scotland

First published in 1988 Conran Octopus Limited
37 Shelton Street, Covent Garden, London WC2H 9HN

ISBN 1 85029 167 5